© 2004 by Barbour Publishing, Inc.

ISBN 1-59310-011-6

Cover image © PhotoDisc

Published by Humble Creek, P.O. Box 719, Uhrichsville, Ohio 44683

Printed in China.
5 4 3 2 1

CONGRATULATIONS

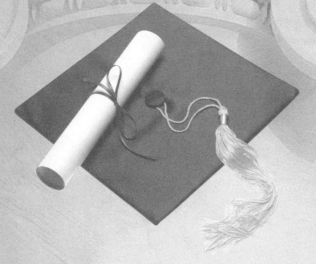

VIOLA RUELKE GOMMER

HUMBLECREEK
INSPIRATION FOR LIFE

*C*ONGRATULATIONS

"I KNOW THE PLANS I HAVE FOR YOU,"

DECLARES THE LORD,

"PLANS TO PROSPER YOU AND NOT TO HARM YOU,

PLANS TO GIVE YOU HOPE AND A FUTURE."

JEREMIAH 29:11 NIV

Congratulations!
It's time to celebrate!
Applause, applause!
Our hats are off to you!
We rejoice in your achievement.

Congratulations!
We offer you a pat on the back.
You have hit the mark.
Well done.
We wish you well.
Let us shake your hand.

Congratulations!
Let's celebrate!
The feast is ready.
The balloons beckon.
The world awaits your gifts and graces.

$\mathcal{C}$ONGRATULATIONS

Congratulations on your achievement.
With every accomplishment, there is an end.
With every end, there is a new beginning.
Life continually moves from a beginning. . .
to an end. . .to a new beginning.

> "No eye has seen, no ear has heard,
> no mind has conceived
> what God has prepared for those who love him."
>
> 1 CORINTHIANS 2:9 NIV

GOD HAS MARVELOUS SURPRISES IN STORE FOR YOU.

> "I am about to do a brand-new thing.
> See, I have already begun!"
>
> ISAIAH 43:19 NLT

$\mathscr{C}$ONGRATULATIONS

Look to your past accomplishments. Acknowledge them. List some of them here:

_____

_____

_____

_____

_____

_____

_____

_____

_____

DON'T LINGER IN THE PAST TOO LONG;
YOU MAY MISS TOMORROW'S OPPORTUNITIES.

While we cherish the past. . .
"We must take from the altar of the past. . .
the fire. . .not the ashes."
A. HERSCHELL

$\mathcal{C}$ONGRATULATIONS

ONLY THAT DAY DAWNS TO WHICH WE ARE AWAKE.

HENRY DAVID THOREAU

What are your plans for this new beginning? Search your heart and your mind. . .then pray for clarity of direction.
Write down the possibilities for your tomorrows.

_____

_____

_____

_____

_____

_____

_____

_____

Use these thoughts and ideas as stepping-stones.
Dare to take the first step.
Seize the moment.
Trust God to guide you as He promised.

$\mathcal{C}$ONGRATULATIONS

And when you turn to the right
or when you turn to the left,
your ears shall hear a word behind you, saying,
"This is the way; walk in it."
ISAIAH 30:21 NRSV

Everything that is full of life loves change,
for the characteristic of life is
movement toward a new goal
and urges toward new pleasures.
BISHOP FULTON SHEEN

NEW GOALS AND NEW PLEASURES AWAIT YOU.

CONGRATULATIONS

As my husband and I left our daughter on the steps of the college dormitory for her freshman year, she handed me an envelope. On the long drive home, I read its contents aloud. My trembling voice gave evidence of my pain at leaving her there. There. . .being a new world. . .a new beginning for her and for us. . . an ending of the known. . .with a new beginning into the unknown.

Let me share with you the gift the envelope contained:

> *Leaving is not simply leaving, not only good-byes, farewells, and benedictions over a time of life that is finished. Leaving is also beginning; it is hello-saying. It is greeting the new dawn that struggles behind darkened clouds of farewell, the dawn being born in brightness and varicolored beauty, enhanced by the clouds of yesterday still lingering in farewell.*
>
> *Beginning and ending are together the moment of dawn, stretching the moment our*

$\mathcal{C}$ONGRATULATIONS

lives take wing and move from place to place,
from people to people, from task to task.
Ending—beginning, changing—becoming,
is the place where in God is.

DWIGHT H. JUDY

I PRAY YOU WILL BE OPEN AND WELCOMING

TO THE NEW TIMES AND NEW PLACES

THAT GOD BECKONS YOU TO ENTER.

God may be invisible,
but He's in touch.
You may not be able to see Him,
but He is in control. . . .
That includes all of life—
past, present, future.

CHARLES SWINDOLL

$\mathcal{C}$ONGRATULATIONS

Albert Einstein wrote,
"Try not to become a success,
but rather try to become a person of value."

Persons of value live lives of—
Integrity, Courage, Perseverance, and Gratitude.
Empowered by such virtues,
you will make a difference in life.
Claim them!

CHAPTER ONE

Integrity

INTEGRITY IS
THE FOUNDATION FOR ALL OTHER VALUES.

*L*ive with Integrity.

Integrity means your life is based on

TRUTH. . .JUSTICE. . .and RIGHT LIVING.

Integrity means you have a conscience and listen to it.

Integrity defines the quality of your life.

Choose integrity and all its challenges.

ℰONGRATULATIONS

I have chosen the way of truth;
I have set my heart on your laws.
PSALM 119:30 NIV

He who walks with integrity walks securely.
PROVERBS 10:9 NKJV

A person of integrity. . .
Speaks the truth.
Owns his actions.
Lives in the light.
Makes commitments.
Is respected.
Keeps promises.
Is other-centered.

The time is always right
to do what is right.
MARTIN LUTHER KING JR.

$\mathscr{C}$ONGRATULATIONS

Beware of the four enemies of integrity:

    Self-interest—Things we want for ourselves.

    Self-protection—Things we don't want or try to avoid.

    Self-deception—A refusal to see a situation clearly or
        as it really is.

    Self-righteousness—An end-justifies-the-means
        attitude.

THE JOHNSON INSTITUTE OF ETHICS

God will help you stay "other-centered"
in your life's journey.
Ask Him.

Jesus said,
"Do to others as you would
have them do to you."
LUKE 6:31 NRSV

ℰongratulations

SEND FORTH YOUR LIGHT

AND YOUR TRUTH,

LET THEM GUIDE ME.

PSALM 43:3 NIV

Some people do things right.
Others do the right thing.
That is integrity.

*D*o all the good you can,

by all the means you can,

in all the ways you can,

in all the places you can,

at all the times you can,

to all the people you can,

as long as ever you can.

JOHN WESLEY

CHAPTER TWO

Courage

COURAGE IS FEAR THAT HAS SAID ITS PRAYERS.

DOROTHY BERNARD

*C*ONGRATULATIONS

WHAT WORRIES YOU MASTERS YOU.
HADDON W. ROBINSON

What worry or worries are masters of you now? Acknowledge them. In God's presence, we dare "name" our demons. Name them by writing them down.

_____

_____

_____

_____

_____

_____

_____

_____

Let him have all your worries and cares,
for he is always thinking about you
and watching everything that
concerns you.

1 PETER 5:7 TLB

*C*ONGRATULATIONS

Mark Twain said,
"Courage is resistance to fear,
master of fear. . .not absence of fear.
Except a creature be part coward it is not
a compliment to say it is brave."

*L*ife is filled with stories of courage. Courage that knew fear, yet moved beyond it to achieve, to discover, to win, to live, to love. I pray that you will acknowledge your fears. I pray that you will stay close to God as you walk to the other side of fear. The other side of fear is courage. There, with God's help, you will achieve, discover, win, live, and love. Your life's struggle will become a story. . .a story of a courageous pilgrim.

*G*od is with you.

He said, "Be strong and courageous.

Do not be terrified;

do not be discouraged,

for the LORD your God

will be with you wherever you go"
(JOSHUA 1:9 NIV).

He will replace your concerns with confidence.

He will offer wisdom in the choices you make.

Trust Him and His promise.

$\mathcal{C}$ONGRATULATIONS

Fear knocked at the door.

Faith answered.

No one was there.

INSCRIPTION ON AN ANCIENT MANTELPIECE
IN HIND'S HEAD HOTEL, BRAY, ENGLAND

Name what you are afraid of today.
Speak it out loud.
Then say, "God is with me;
I will not be afraid.
He will give me courage.
He will *be* my courage."
Greet each new day with
this statement of truth.
Believe it with all your heart.
It will carry you through
the most difficult times.

CONGRATULATIONS

TO CONQUER FEAR IS THE BEGINNING OF WISDOM.

BERTRAND RUSSELL

I sought the LORD,
and he answered me,
and delivered me from all my fears.

PSALM 34:4 NRSV

CHAPTER THREE

Perseverance

GREAT WORKS ARE PERFORMED
NOT BY STRENGTH
BUT BY PERSEVERANCE.

SAMUEL JOHNSON

Congratulations

Nothing in this world can take the place of persistence. Talent will not; nothing is more common than unsuccessful people with talent. Genius will not; unrewarded genius is almost a proverb. Education will not; the world is full of educated derelicts. Persistence and determination alone are omnipotent. The slogan "press on" has solved and always will solve the problems of the human race.

Calvin Coolidge

*C*ONGRATULATIONS

TEN RULES OF PERSISTENCE:

1. Fall seven times. Stand up eight. (JAPANESE PROVERB)

2. See failure as just another way of doing something.

3. Know that there are no shortcuts to success.

4. Never quit.

5. Want to succeed? Double your failure rate. (THOMAS WATSON)

6. Slow and steady wins the race. (AESOP)

7. Never try to look back and move forward at the same time.

8. Don't argue for your limitations; you'll get to keep them. (RICHARD BACH)

9. Be opportunity minded.

10. Try one more time.

I CAN DO EVERYTHING THROUGH HIM
WHO GIVES ME STRENGTH.

PHILIPPIANS 4:13 NIV

CONGRATULATIONS

Our energy is in proportion to
the resistance it meets.
We attempt nothing great,
but from a sense of the difficulties
we have to encounter,
we persevere in nothing great,
but from a pride in overcoming them.

WILLIAM HAZLITT

AS YOUR DAYS, SO IS YOUR STRENGTH.

DEUTERONOMY 33:25 NRSV

Congratulations

ONE IS DEFEATED ONLY WHEN ONE ACCEPTS DEFEAT.

MARSHALL FOCH

Do not throw away your confidence;
it will be richly rewarded.
You need to persevere so that when
you have done the will of God,
you will receive what he has promised.

HEBREWS 10:35–36 NIV

Congratulations

"TAKE COURAGE!

DO NOT LET YOUR HANDS BE WEAK,

FOR YOUR WORK SHALL BE REWARDED."

2 Chronicles 15:7 nrsv

Be patient with everyone,
but above all with thyself.
I mean, do not be disheartened
by your imperfections,
but always rise up with fresh courage.
St. Francis de Sales

CHAPTER FOUR

Gratitude

NOTHING IS MORE HONORABLE THAN A GRATEFUL HEART.

SENECA

*C*ONGRATULATIONS

No matter what accomplishments you have achieved, someone helped you.

ALTHEA GIBSON

I URGE YOU, FIRST OF ALL,

TO PRAY FOR ALL PEOPLE. . .

AND GIVE THANKS.

1 TIMOTHY 2:1 NLT

$\mathscr{C}$ONGRATULATIONS

In ordinary life we hardly realize that we receive a great deal more than we give, and that it is only with gratitude that life becomes rich.

DIETRICH BONHOEFFER

How rich is your life with gifts received? Think of times, places, experiences, and people who have been gifts to you. Name them on the lines below.

_____

_____

_____

_____

_____

_____

_____

_____

_____

_____

_____

OFFER A PRAYER OF THANKSGIVING FOR EACH REMEMBERED GIFT.

CONGRATULATIONS

ACCEPT MY THOUGHTS FOR THANKS, I HAVE NO WORDS.

HANNAH MORE

The bell rang signaling the end of the school day. The students stood in line at the classroom door in alphabetical order. My name began with "R." I was close to the end of the line. Mr. Weiss handed each student the appropriate science project folder. An eternity passed.

Finally, I stood before Mr. Weiss. As he handed me the project folder, he said, "Please wait for me by my desk." My heart stopped. Somehow I moved toward his desk. I waited. At long last all the other students had left the room. Mr. Weiss came to where I stood. He turned to me and said, "Your project is the best I have ever received for this assignment. Some of the other students asked to see it. I hope you don't mind that I shared it with them. They were in awe!"

I don't think I had taken a breath since he asked me to wait by his desk. Did I hear him right? Did he say it was the best? I took a breath and said, "May I ask you a question?" He shook his head yes. "Please

*C*ONGRATULATIONS

tell me what 'awe' means." Wonder, admiration was his response. I thanked him and began to leave. Then he spoke these words, "I am in awe of your work too. Keep it up. I am proud of you."

I wish I could whisper in your ear. . . *Thank you, Mr. Weiss.* Over the years my heart has often said thank you.

THOUGH MY MOUTH BE DUMB,
MY HEART SHALL THANK YOU.
NICHOLAS ROWE

Gratitude is
the memory of the heart.
JEAN BAPTISTE MASSIEU

I thank my God every time
I remember you.
PHILIPPIANS 1:3 NRSV

*C*ONGRATULATIONS

ONE CAN NEVER PAY IN GRATITUDE;

ONE CAN ONLY PAY "IN KIND"

SOMEWHERE ELSE IN LIFE.

ANNE MORROW LINDBERGH

*C*ONGRATULATIONS

WITHOUT THE ASSISTANCE OF THE DIVINE BEING. . .

I CANNOT SUCCEED.

WITH THAT ASSISTANCE, I CANNOT FAIL.

ABRAHAM LINCOLN

Oh do not pray for easy lives.

Pray to be strong men and women.

Do not pray for tasks equal to your powers.

Pray for powers equal to your tasks.

Then the doing of your work will be no miracle;

but you shall be the miracle.

Every day you shall wonder at yourself,

at the richness of life which has come to you

by the grace of God.

PHILLIPS BROOKS

CONGRATULATIONS

I remember those happy days
and often wish I could speak
into the ears of the dead
the gratitude which was due to them
in life and so ill returned.

GWYN THOMAS

*Y*ou have achieved so much. Don't fail to thank those who have mentored you. Don't allow Gwyn Thomas's words of regret to become yours. Take some time, make a phone call, write a note, make a visit, send a simple gift to those people who have impacted your life with their words, their presence, or their listening ear. It is time to say, "You have helped to make me who I am and what I am. . .a person of value."

$\mathscr{C}$ONGRATULATIONS

Resources for your mind and heart as you continue on life's journey:

ANDREWS, ANDY	*The Traveler's Gift*
CARTER-SCOTT, CHERIE	*If Life Is a Game, These Are the Rules*
EDELMAN, MARIAN WRIGHT	*The Measure of Our Success*
MAXWELL, JOHN C.	*Success: One Day at a Time*
MOTHER TERESA	*Meditations from a Simple Path*
NOUWEN, HENRI J. M.	*Bread for the Journey*

Other resources:

_____

_____

_____

_____

_____

_____

$\mathcal{C}$ONGRATULATIONS

Be yourself;
no base imitator of another,
but your best self.
There is something which
you can do better than another.
Listen to the inward voice
and bravely obey that.
Do the things at which you are great,
not what you were never made for.
RALPH WALDO EMERSON

Love Mom + Richard

ONCE MORE,

CONGRATULATIONS ON

YOUR ACHIEVEMENT!